Collected F-

ADAM JOHNSON was born in 1965 in Stalybridge, Cheshire. In 1984 he moved to London, where he worked for the BBC, a theatre-booking agency and a reference-book publisher. As early as 1986, he self-published a pamphlet of poems, *In the Garden*. His later work appeared in magazines, anthologies, and three collections: *Poems* (Hearing Eye, 1992), *The Spiral Staircase* (Acumen, 1993) and *The Playground Bell* (Carcanet, 1994). He died in May 1993.

NEIL POWELL, born in London in 1948, has taught English, owned a bookshop and, since 1990, been a full-time author and editor; he lives in Suffolk. His Carcanet books include five collections of poetry – *At the Edge* (1977), *A Season of Calm Weather* (1982), *True Colours* (1991), *The Stones on Thorpeness Beach* (1994) and *Selected Poems* (1998) – as well as *Carpenters of Light* (1979), *Roy Fuller: Writer and Society* (1995) and *The Language of Jazz* (1997). His *George Crabbe: An English Life* will appear in 2004.

ADAM JOHNSON

Collected Poems

Edited with an Afterword by Neil Powell

CARCANET

First published in 2003 by
Carcanet Press Limited
Alliance House
Cross Street
Manchester M2 7AQ

A CIP catalogue record for this book
is available from the British Library

ISBN 978 1 8575 4637 8

The publisher acknowledges financial assistance
from the Arts Council of England

Set in Monotype Garamond by XL Publishing Services, Tiverton
Printed and bound in England by SRP Ltd, Exeter

Contents

Editorial Note

Between November 1985, when I met him, and his death in May 1993, Adam Johnson sent or gave me a signed and dated copy of almost every poem he wrote. In all but a handful of cases, the texts printed here are based on a comparison of those original typescripts and any final published versions which exist: in the later poems, there are seldom any significant differences, though in a few of the earlier pieces I have had to make an editorial choice between the freshness of a first version and the polish of a revision. Otherwise, my editorial interventions have been as minimal as possible, essentially confined to correcting obvious slips of punctuation and spelling. Single dates given are those of each poem's completion, where this is known: sometimes, of course, a piece might have been worked on for months (or, in a couple of cases, years) before reaching this stage, but as a rule Adam moved swiftly from the creative occasion to the finished poem. A small number of undated typescripts have been placed where they seem best to belong, taking into account theme and style as well as any circumstantial evidence – such as the machine they were typed on or where they landed in my file. I have excluded fragments, false starts, two very early pieces and also one poem ('On the Coach') which Adam began in 1986 and revised in 1992: he remained dissatisfied with this and, in its hybrid state, it seems to belong among neither the earlier nor the later work; moreover, its ideas are re-used in other, better poems. Otherwise, there is very little recycling, even from poems which remained unpublished during Adam's lifetime: the most notable exception is the reappearance of three lines from 'Heavy my Gold-ball Baby' in the retrospective 'In the Garden', which incorporates a good deal of previously-drafted material.

Any further analytical introduction would, I think, simply get in the way of an extraordinary poetic journey; but for readers who would like to know a little more about Adam I have included as an Afterword a slightly revised version of the short obituary memoir I wrote for *PN Review* in 1993.

The editor and publisher wish to record their grateful thanks to Joyce Johnson for sanctioning this edition and to Patricia Oxley of Acumen for permission to reprint poems from *The Spiral Staircase* (Acumen, 1993).

N.P.

1985

After Hours

Night pales,
Voiceless, in the grave
Of love's cold corpses,
Dead as dreams.

Alone now, as before,
The young men fled,
Dark the place
Where fancy bred,
And there by the black walls
Where the faint heart bled;
Pretty painted faces
With promiscuous smiles –
Too late, love passed by
Disguised.

And there, on the sad, dark street,
Youth cherishes his misery.
In love with being in love,
He drinks; nourishing his soul.

How wise, for one of seventeen!
How brave! How beautiful!
How pitiful,
The tragedy of truth.

1984–May 1985

I of Glass

I seem to fascinate him.
Such furtive glances,
From one who claims
That he has nothing more
To hide –
There is little remaining
For those weary eyes,
In me.
Or does he hope to find
A new face here?

I do not welcome many smiles
These days.

He checks his image.
Who is he
Trying to please?
I am not famous
For my compliments.

Quick!
Someone buy him
Another beer,
For time is running out,
And there is still no promise
Of a coffee tonight.

Perhaps the lonely blond
Will yet be his –
But can he still afford
Free love?

I have no pity left
For him.
Too long, I have framed
The sad reflections,
Of men whose names
Are fading
On the lavatory wall.

September 1985

Viewers' Guide to the Office

Nine a.m.
In the office,
Here they come
With the TV page,
Brains washed clean
With soap,
Ready for Monday's
Viewing report.

A busy weekend
By the box;
They all saw that movie –
So very true to life,
And culture
From America –
On every channel!

What a treat.

It's the serial tonight,
They'll be staying in
For that,
And the video is ready,
Just in case ...

They are normal,
Happy people,
But they look on me
With narrow minds:

Their view of the world
Is only twenty-two
Inches wide.

To a Raven

A raven perched
Upon an ancient oak,
There to contemplate
His ominous existence,
And made enquiry
Of his host:
'What know you
Of this wretched world?'

From its cracked
And creaking midst,
The oak despaired:

'Oh carrion bird,
I am all but dead,
Behold! My grotesque paralysis!
And from this
Drably shrouded girth,
Strike black, disfigured bones.

I have seasoned
In these summers,
As they rise and writhe
In this wreckage
Of broken boughs,
My roots drain
The misery of man;
His legacy,
My leafy cerements bear.
The stinking corpses
Of his guilt,
Bleed poison in the earth –
This great necropolis,
And I, replete,
Will mark his sepulchre.

In my death,
I will find no sleep;
When from bloody clouds
His children weep,
A rain of burning tears,
In mourning
Of man's vain, mortal hope.
That little god,
With dreams of fire,
Behold him now!
All blistery-backed,
And flesh, charring
In the pyre.'

Silently,
The slate-winged bird
Went skyward,
And the only light
Was in the ebon shining
Of his eyes.

October–November 1985

Curious Place

A curious place this,
And like so very many
We have seen before.

Exclusive of course,
And popular as ever
With the old crowd.

All types here, something
For everybody. We wear
Our keys on both sides.

Here we can be proud of our
Individuality –
See, each moustache is quite

Unique. And down in
The cellar bar,
In ultraviolet shadows,

A familiar face.
We've met him often. He
Remains anonymous.

His identity is skin tight.

July–December 1985

Posy

They sit at their favourite table
By the artificial ferns. A posy

Of perfumed boys, smooth and slender
In their summer plumage. They share

A cigarette and remember
The lovers who have filled their ashtrays.

Listen, they have much to say
For here, in this and other

Such sophisticated bars,
They have seen much of life and know

The value of freedom. They all
Wear their mascara with pride.

July–December 1985

Under Ground

Insensible, we seep
Under ground into
The people-sewer that warms
With a city's stale breath;
Down the dry artery,
A turmoil of legs
That work entirely

Independent of the brain.
In angular confinement,
Conscious only of hands,
Wait sleepy sentinels
(All tickets must be shown).
Descent is all we know:
The toy-like clanging

Of the escalator
On the long jostle to the track.
Boarding the westbound
In the stench of human meat,
A ritual odour, we orgy
In our sweating knot,
Not quite intimate.

And the worm rattles on.
On through the tangling bowel,
The grimy excavations
Of metropolitan man,
To the same destination –
Another London station.
We spill out; the subway gapes.

Clean air sneaks in
And loiters, a stranger.
Up, up then to the street,
Squinting like rats
Unaccustomed to the light.
And still we fail to see
What it illuminates.

November–December 1985

Dead Leaves, Dead Year

Dead leaves, dead year, bruising
In the graceful grass. December
Recalls the semen smell

Of autumn. In the slumped bramble,
Naked but for the thorns
Its hidden nests, slow

Beetles await the frost.
Ice makes cataracts.
The quiet pool is blind.

December 1985

1986

It is What we Wanted, Isn't It?

It is what we wanted, isn't it?

Though he does not surround me
with the tender radiance
of your skin,

though this hard dry member
is not the gentle tool
that fed my frailer body
with your love,

and though, when morning comes,
he will not understand me,

it must be right;

it is what we wanted, isn't it?

February 1986

Leather Guise

The blue pinspot
shafts, smoke-grained
onto black leather.

Its smashed beam
flounders
on a multitude of skins,

pulsing; the rhythm
of securely zippered
maleness.

Peaks worn low, unsmiling,
they cruise the bar –
the leather guys,

who advertise
fidelity, integrity,
in all the current magazines –

'No time-wasters please!
No fats, no skinnies,
and *no* effeminates!'

Meanwhile, glistening
in a nitrate haze,
posing to his very best
advantage –

feet firm and wide apart,
he stands and drinks
straight from the can.

Being gay is serious business,
when you're a leather man.

February–April 1986

Sea Chant

Alone, in the long embrace
　　　of Ringstead Bay,
I sit down and listen
　　　to the sea.

Some distance off,
Across its shifting acres,
A spangled sun slick
Dances out, quick flashes,
Sparks, white hot on
　　　liquid lead,
Borne coastward
In the breaker's curling
　　　scoop.

The sea's white lip incantates,
Forming distinct vowel sounds
That echo up the long drool,
Never quite a word.

I put my hands into
　　　the slobbering sea;
Thrust the deep shingle –
Its loose, wet heaviness
Of innumerable tiny stones,
Like parti-coloured teeth,
Sleek as baby skin.

Sea chant. The shrill laughter
Stones make, as each wave
Invigorates.

The cliff's jaw cuts the sky,
Rupturing slate,
Disgorging light that strikes
　　　the gull's head,
Like a gloriole.

Earth beats under me –
My body, a filament; blood and bone,
Alive with the sea, Life,
Pulsing in my flesh,
Or driving its charge
Through earth, through rock –
Resounding in the great sea shout,

Ever … ever!

Sea chant. Song of life,
My spirit beats with you.

April 1986

Forsythia

The sun's proboscis
Pierces the nebula,
Tasting stars.

Flowers sing with light,
Hung, like bright insects,
In the webbing thorns.

First petals grasp for air,
Baptised by the sun.

April 1986

Moonchild

Breathless, the wood arches its rib.
Light, blobbed up in its ferny cleavage,
Slithers under, dragging night,
A plethora of stars.

Heaved up against the sky,
Trees cut their tattered edge,
Bullied by the moon, as

Moon-sick, one thin cloud
Lifts its limb, baring gristle.

Rat waits clenched in the dark,
While, stricken by its quickshot eye,
A child burns,
Whispering the name
Of his desire.

June 1986

Symphonia

Shostakovich: Symphony No. 8

I wake in the earth.
Over, over I turn,
My mouth full of soil;
Under my lip,
The teeth ground out –
My tongue cuts
On a silent shout.

> Enough room to scrape
>   with one claw,
> But not to turn my eyes
> As earth scours out,
> With black, choking grains,
> The bright anxieties of light.

I spin faster in the dark.
Sudden shock of muscle:
The worm bites,
Sensing a pulse.

I yield, to the music
Of its suck.

June 1986

26 June 1986

It is summer, and here, upon a bench
which lazes on the rise of this
city park, I sit, unspecial in
the easy scene.

Nearby, a boy reclines, shirtless in
the shadow-fingering of leaves.
He is writing, as I am writing;
and suddenly, the intimacy
of this moment brings to me
an image of our unity –
though we shall never touch,
and he will never know my name.

June 1986

A Haven of Listening

for Robin Bone

Outside, the evening has happened,
So deftly, I hadn't noticed.
Music comes as a diversion
From the poem's intransigence;
Concerto in G by Ravel
(Though the room retains a feel of
The Romantic). Thought startles wrist,
The second movement commences,
Adagio assai. Its key
Is E Major, introspective,
A sustained nocturne. So very apt.

We both have come to know this room,
Our temporary domicile,
And I, though more a stranger here,
Find myself accustomed to its
Timeless, comfortable chaos.
Here, for a while, we have escaped:
No brash intrusions to defile
The luxury of quietude, in
This, our haven of listening.
Let us look forward to the time
When ways to another will be mapped.

July 1986

Egg

Sun is crying – red agonies
That sting the white eye of morning.

One tear lands on the snail,
Filling his coil with God-pus.

The snail does not believe in God –
He knows that it is Earth which

Replenishes his meal of leaves
And works his foot.

A starling splices the mollusc.
She loves God every morning with her beak

And knows that God is in the snail.
Sun's tear explodes against her wing.

Her egg shudders in the womb,
Anticipating life.

July 1986

Evening Meal

Continent of back gardens,
Hung out on the Pennine sheet.

The air is an interfusion –
Gnat-blown and stove-heavy.

A dog's mood is the yard's length,
Dead-newt-smell of potato peelings
Wet on its breath.

Tea's

ready.

The whole planet stops, gape-mouthed,
Huddled under the table.

July 1986

Dancers

for Mother

You dance on the high edge of a star,
　　Its regions glisten. You coalesce,
　　Bright atoms that spin a silverness –
Set free, partnered by the air you are.

The ballroom; a lit space where you trot
　　Your slow-foxing legato – to music
　　Which affords a graceful eurhythmic –
Sacred this place, though partners are not.

You are inextinguishable light.
　　One quick step is often all it takes;
　　Your wing, sequined, is the joy it makes,
Starlike now, you trace a dance, a night.

July–August 1986

Bluebottle

Little motorised bead, you are
A beast of remarkable stupidity –
Insisting as you do on that
Illegible aerial scrawl. How can this,
A very navigable space,
Confound even so unreasoning a brain?

Too late! I am bored with this game.
You ricochet, land at last on the curtain.
Under my aimed swipe, you split on its fabric,
A small coal; a cooling fragment.

Chaotic, iridescent thing,
Looking at your smashed body I remember
Our existence is relative.

September 1986

The Book of Lies

In a corner of
The bookshop lurks
The book of lies.

The Children's Bible,
This, its latest guise,
And a reminder of

How well the poison works;
Getting at the youth
Before they realise

That theirs is the right
To choose the truth.

November 1986

Nocturne

October makes censers
Of these wooded places.
Out of the cool ether
Of darkness strike the
Branching crystals of trees,
By night's definition
Of a rarer substance –
The texture of bark
Is wholly light's privilege.

The path leads us to
A locked gate we climb. There is
Tension in our nearness –
The feel of you, our hands
Clasped in recognition
Of their own engaged warmth.

In embracing we earth,
Here, where a stream's course
Through banks of cypresses
Designs a garden,
The motion of its cool blade
As purposeful as blood.

Now the spell of your voice
Concedes to other sound,
Falling into dark air
That cherishes each note –
This water easing
Over known rocks, through reeds,
The soft consent of leaves.
Drawing me close, there is
Nothing you would not give.

December 1986

1987

Lines on a Postcard

for Ivor C. Treby

Curvaceous, the supple line
That softness lifts untextured
To his eye. Touching that skin,
More firm beneath his hand,
He senses a radiance
Which is much more of them both,
Than their mutual desire.

June 1987

Rain

Defined, consistency is rain.
Such love as rivulets retain,
Runs deepest where its roots remain;
A kind of booze to dull the brain,
Proficient in the ease of pain.

Date unknown

Discovery

How misinterpreted is light perceived
In one who recognises only surfaces:
    Light that is reflected
Does not necessarily retain
The quality of illumination.

Date unknown

Making

for Montana Silkwood

The life you inhabit
Is inherent with the same
Light, by which you fashion
Each requisite habit.
No perquisite of fame
Inspiring your passion,

But a sense of fun,
Money enough to live,
And the love of making.
In this, we both have one
Imperative: to give
All to the undertaking.

Both poem and costume
Are means of expression;
Implicit in each,
An image we assume.
I learn my profession –
The exactitude of speech

(With sensitivity,
By an established craft).
To keep the pattern true,
I strive for clarity:
Through each draft and re-draft,
In making this for you

Whose bearing is easy;
The attitude of one
Civilised by travel.
And innately unprosy,
By your own conviction,
An individual.

It is thus we achieve
True communication;
One clear light for the sake
Of all that we believe.
This is our liberation,
And that of all we make.

Date unknown

1988

The Fire

for Neil Powell

And yes, we grow ironic as we learn:
Bland hope, lit by the truth, condemns the fool –
Whose fear of reason bids him pass the time
With fools – who, as all men, must die alone.
His word is branded with an insane fire:
Keep faith without conviction – ethics lie.

Trust in the senses, or condone the lie –
Religions, like policemen, never learn.
The road to freedom leaves a trail of fire,
Which all must follow blindly with the fool.
And he that travels, travels best alone,
In owing nothing but his place in time.

And yes, we have the best of worlds. In time
Each gift assumes the pattern of a lie –
Man cannot live by happiness alone,
The mirror shows us more than we would learn:
The patriot will recognise the fool,
Naked with him in liberty and fire.

The poet's hand commands a living fire
That feeds the burning currency of time:
Exactitude and form dissolve the lie
That politicians weave. For every fool
A government exists. The more we learn,
We learn to keep the flame that burns alone.

A star flares to the touch. Not love alone
But loyalty is tested in its fire.
We reach and reach for what we cannot learn
As critics come and go. Great in their time,
True to their trade, forgive them when they lie –
Only the just have leave to judge the fool.

Deep in the eye of man, perceive a fool
Whose vision is unique. In him alone
Does fear of death give credence to the lie
That to his end Salvation bends its fire.
Hope marks his grave – the shoveller is time:
Interred therein, all he will ever learn.

And yet, the swiftest envoy is the fool,
Who walks the darkened watershed alone:
His words are dressed with roses, but they lie.

January 1988

Inside

for Maurice Douay

Here are moments cool with sleep,
where no words are, nor the smallest
gesture unloved – time beyond us
and within us, we lie within touch
and are not afraid.
           Light like air
falls across the sheet, shadow
of glass: the same light which through
leaves moves in the shape of leaves –
light composed of the memory of light,
ghost in the leaf.
           See, it has found us:
our hands respond, gentlest of strangers,
and your touch, love, is a razor.

Sunflower Harvest

for Graham and Jeremy

Fast roads dissect a landscape
Of tall girls with ruined fringes.
Redundant stalks assume the shape
Each seed compelled, whose root estranges:

Sunflower harvest and a season cast,
Kilometres of heavy vines
Stand rude with fruit. We know at last
That only space itself confines

This region to our field of vision.
Light, topography and motion prove
Our sense of freedom an illusion:
Not how or why but that we move.

And should we arrive, and if we return,
Arriving and returning are the same errand:
We learn in ourselves what sunflowers learn,
Heads bowed, in deference to the land.

November 1988

The Night Ferry

for Colin Hunter

Wherever we must home to (even via
  the port of Dover where the English
perfected the art of delay) it is worth noting
  that going back accounts for
less time at sea than does an outward voyage –
  or seemingly:
                    perhaps
a sense of the inevitable – work,
  the post, the awful news –
merely restores to us the familiar topography
  of the place we keep our days in,
where even strangers talk in our own language –
  though rarely after dawn
in a public bar.
                    (On the Warmoesstraat,
  in a quarter of the city
whose every portal is hospitable,
  we have discussed the universe
with gods who drink *jenever* with their breakfast.)
  Whether our peregrinations
are solitary or made with one we trust
  will keep us from being bored
between lunch and dinner, a last evening encroaches.
  And now, a mile or so
off shore, alone, still fairly drunk, I stand,
  look back across the stern
to where Zeebrugge is a slick of lights
  anonymous among
the coded stars, and think of every face,
  awed by the same night,
whose mouth 'O's with the names of continents –
  Boredom and Loneliness.
Freedom in transit, then – at a given instant
  not to be anywhere?
But this unhomely vessel is no time machine –
  land, though not in sight,
lies dead ahead.
                    We'll turn our watches back,
    glad if we have been missed,
and go together down St Martin's Lane.

Date unknown

The Bunker

Eulogy on the Brief Encounter, St Martin's Lane, London
for Richard Pyatt

All for whom solace is
A room of strangers, bless
The Bunker – mise-en-scène
Of prime locality,
Where stylish thugs convene
With ordinary gods,
Exchanging histories
In an intimate cellar.
Subterraneous,
Nearer therefore to Mother,
Descending from the street
Into its relative gloom,

Upon us are conferred
All the comforts of the womb.
Across the bar we meet
The quick praise of the strange
Complicity inferred
In practised half-smiles, nods:
These are unambiguous,
Wearing no mysteries.
Clerk, philosopher and lover
Must call the god to blame,
Certain in their exchange
Of being unheard. The same

Gestures, the coded word,
Preserve an ancient rite,
United in our theme,
Though differently blessed,
We share a common need
And the collective stare:
Regard us as you might
With healthy interest,
Touch, gently, if you dare –
Touch, see how we bleed.
We love therefore we are
No less than what we seem.

December 1988

Carol

for John Heath-Stubbs

The needles are all bristling on the pine
And roots that strike beneath clutch in the snow,
Soft light beyond the trees returns the glow
Illumined in the amber of your wine.

Something has begun. You would divine
The echo that began an age ago:
Clear splinters in the pane begin to show
The spirit of the glass incarnadine.

Bright sluice of blood that courses through the ox
Whose shivers waken fury in the ass,
The watchful child whose fingers in the box

Distress the brittle icicles of grass,
In searching for the gift finds only rocks.
What consolation? Spring may come to pass.

December 1988

1989

Waiting for When you Wake

for Jim

Waiting for when you wake,
Stranger to breath that comes
Over the unstirred leaves,
     Or those red skies
That by their rarity
Sustain you in dreamed flight –
I, corporeal merely,
     Love you dearly.

If at the mercy of an ache,
Prey to the flesh that drums,
Or light that falls in sheaves
     To press closed eyes,
Ruthless in its charity –
If waking comes too bright,
Will you, who contain the sky,
     Teach me to fly?

January 1989

Yes

His answer came unbidden to her pain:
     The breathless word
Delivered her to sleep.
     He wept, unheard,
At what he could not keep,
Arose and went outside into the rain.

January 1989

31

Road to Arisaig

Mountain rock will make no bargain with us —
Disdainful at our interest, pulling its shoulders
Into a shrug of granite. Only the rain argues,
With its politics of tactical erosion,
As we, the less consistent, by this thoroughfare
Gain access to the sea: we shall not stay

Nor are committed to return this way.
And mountain rock makes no bargain with us —
Clenching our history in a weathered fist,
As sure of its hold as it is without pity,
Which has too friable a quality:
Here we are nothing less than irrelevant —

We lose our footing with each step we take,
Each act a new acknowledgement of failure —
How shall we reason when love has renounced us?
Where can we go now we have gone too far?
Time overtakes us knowing all our destinations —
A cold chisel writing our names in stone.

February 1989

For your Birthday

(Robin)

This, by birth-right, is your day —
From its sheath the Martian sword
Drags a blade of molten stars.

Aries, in his blazing fleece,
Decks the Spring about his horns
And wakened by his drunken jigs,

Fervid shoots embrace the sun
Ripened in the temperate soil —
Treasure these, your vernal gifts,

These folded manuscripts of light:
May Bacchus ever tend your cup,
Bright Ariel, your every wish,

And, dear, on this memorial night
As all the constellations burn
I toast you with the wine of love.

March 1989

Villanelle

Each man is guilty in his brothers' eyes,
Brought by his father to a graceless state.
Granted remission only when he dies,

Craving fulfilment, weeping as he tries –
Alone, the victim of his human trait,
Each man is guilty in his brothers' eyes

And values most what every hand denies.
He learns adversity, each wound innate,
Granted remission only when he dies.

A disingenuous character belies
The shame no abstract love will compensate:
Each man is guilty in his brothers' eyes.

Compassion guarantees no compromise,
Nor comforts him who teaches men to hate –
Granted remission only when he dies,

He rises to embrace and, laughing, cries:
'I loved you after all.' It comes too late:
Each man is guilty in his brothers' eyes,
Granted remission only when he dies.

21 April 1989

December 1989

The nascent winter turns
Each root into a nail,
And in the West there burns
A sun morbid and pale.

Now, from the city bars
We drift, into a cool
Gymnasium of stars –
The drunkard and the fool:

Into the night we go,
Finding our separate ways –
The darkness fraught with snow,
The leaves falling like days.

December 1989

1990

The Artifact

for Stephen Spender

The map of thought –
A landscape in relief
Traversed by roads:
Conviction, disbelief,

Integrity
Convergent in the act –
Word within word,
Essential, artifact.

March 1990

Sunbather

Who lies all afternoon
Rocked in its balm of sun,
A touch imbued with heat
That covers him with light,
Hears all about him tolled
The ringing of the world –

Communities that sing
Or vibrate where they hang,
Sheer weight of earth beneath,
Insistence of the breath –
The eyes hard and immense
As blue after distance.

13 May 1990

Birthday Song for the Twenty-Sixth of May

for Staiszu Lovendoski

For this, your birthday, I invoke
Two Mercurial and airy dancers –
Those restless empyreal Twins –
To run beside you everywhere:

Eloquent messengers they are, who bring
Felicitations of pavonian Juno.
Each also bears, in either hand,
Love's quicksilver and Maia's emerald.

May 1990

Silence

What is this novel sense that, as I stand,
    An axle in the reeling world,
      Has made absurd
    The drumming of the blood?

What has this absence in the day revealed?
    Charged with the violence of a word,
      It hurts the ear
    Because it makes no sound.

June 1990

The Spiral Staircase

for Sandeha

I

    Halfway down the stairs that curl
Headlong toward an inconstant circle,
Midway between air and light that lied
And the dispassionate darkness, inherit
A sense. From here the way is easy –
See how the path steepens away,
How much easier it is to breathe.
Turn again – this was your window,
These your things.
                The last flame quickens,
Voices push at the thick curtains,
Light passes and is extinguished.

II

    Alone now as before, when under
An outraged sky you stood at the watershed
(Remember Black Hill, North Grain, Ringing Roger)
Drawing no sustenance from acid peat,
Finding the fruit rotted under wet leaves
Where the scavenging wasp unsheathes its needle –
    Remember that child in a garden in April
Forcing the whorled calyx of a rose,
Turning a stone where the beetle shelters,
Trying the soil with ravenous fingers –
What root flourished that you did not kill?
    Child with the net and the killing jar,
What was your grievance?
                Vanessa atalanta,
Marbled guest of the stinging nettle,
Beware the approach of the Northern winter –
Mother your progeny deep in the patch
Where curious children dare not enter.

III

Halfway down the spiral stairs,
Midway between air and light that lied
And the dispassionate darkness, turn again.
Here is a bed of weeds – your memory.
                    And was it here
That you knew the bite of the garden spider?
Wrote your epitaph on the moving leaves?
                Time for a game of hide-and-seek –
Deep in the willow-herb no one will find you
(Listen, the pursuers' footsteps recede).
Turn again.
                    A voice behind you
(Was it your own voice or the alarm
'Pink pink' of the paranoiac bird?):
                                'Come with me,
It is not far to Bleaklow Hill,
The root is well marked out with stakes.'
Remember, from here the way is easy.

IV

          Heartland – a high place between rivers.
Pause at the tumulus, this covered barrow,
Hlew sacred to the ancient hunters,
Gritstone plateau of the first Pecsaeten,
Royal forest of the Norman invaders –
How shall you follow them into the wilderness?
                    But this is not the place.
          Nor will you walk on Batham Gate
Into Anavio.
                    Make no pilgrimage
To the curative springs of AQVE ARNEMETIAE,
Leave your rushes at the Forest Chapel,
Your frame of petals by Mompesson's Well
(Come Plague Sunday the clay will dry) –
Turn, knowing this is not the place.
                Stand on the bridge by Panniers Pool
Where three shires meet at the running border,
A constant boundary in perpetual motion:
Witness, if you have the time, the insidious
Redefinition of the feeder's course,
This random displacement of detritus.

By virtue of an insouciant mineral force,
You are where you were and you are here also
In another county.
                    It is not the place,
Yet, without knowing, you were nearest in the act –
In that one instant as you crossed the river
And entered the place that was not either.

V

        Alone now as before
Halfway down the stairs that curl
Headlong toward an inconstant circle,
Turn for the last time.
                    Remember
From here the way is easy.

June 1990

The Gift

*for Don Bachardy
on the Last Drawings of Christopher Isherwood*

In work that loved the eye was merciless –
Catching its subject in the act of death –
But read consent between the lines of pain
And from decay construed its otherness:

Here is the black word drawn under the breath –
Painted to light, veracious and humane –
Motive and consummation in our art
Who live uncertain of its certain terms.

Should our chief dread incite us to reprove
The draughtsman for his honesty, we start
To counter all that artifact affirms –
For not to censor is an act of love.

24 June 1990

View from the Monument

Take the three hundred and eleven stairs
(There is no lift), observing as you climb
The nature of the spiral – that it dares
Contest the uniformity of time –

Such eccentricities are why we came:
Wren's Monument – a city's ancient grief
That smoulders in a copper vase of flame,
And Cibber's allegorical relief.

An urban panorama now affords
The true perspective of a vicious age.
The streets we name are nothing more than words
That read in valediction from the page:

Old Jewry, Savage Gardens, Pudding Lane –
Enduring in the wake of enterprise
They cower in the shadow of the crane.
Like ranks of weeds the gleaming towers rise:

Encroaching on our vision, they abuse
More than the level aspect of the sky.
Each, from below, the grasping magnate views –
Theirs are our cities, though the cities die.

February 1989–July 1990

A Toast

for John Heath-Stubbs on his birthday

A kite of birds blown up the sky
On currents of your imagery

Will know Diana's precinct soon
And glamour of that *clair de lune*,

As wealth of her eburnean light
Illuminates your birthday night –

Unreal cities turn below
Whose voices wake us, that we know

In each, their bright ethereal pubs,
This loving toast – to John Heath-Stubbs.

July 1990

Fear

Through every layer of tar and stone
            The lethal roots extend,
In slow corruption of the walls
            No mason can defend –

Analogies of flesh and bone!
            But what do they portend?
The terror of a love that calls
            And cannot find its friend?

6 September 1990

Poem for the Nineteenth of October

for my mother

After September's embers lazing
    Weld the stamens in the rose,
And leaves that twist and hang amazing
    Grow profound in their repose;
As equinoctial brilliance renders
    Every form in deeps and golds,
A sybaritic Venus tenders
    Gifts of love October holds:
With arabesques in halls of air,
    This naked daughter of the sky
Be partnered with you everywhere,
    Who dances for she cannot die.

October 1990

For Graham Storey

on his seventieth birthday, 8 November 1990

Pluto, by no means a reveller
(Even the cancan's bawdy chthonic reel
Has grave Persephone calling him to heel),
Bears to you on the wings of Aquilla
His birthday greetings. What he shall intone is:
Yours is the provenance of *cor scorpionis*.

Dynamic septuagenarian that you are,
Accept this gift: the constant trust of those
Who praise your cooking and admire your prose –
Roadworthy relic in your Phoebean car –
While stellar eagles guide us from above,
Through the wide sierras of our human love.

November 1990

Table Manners

for Paul Gambaccini

I had forgotten that: the way
Your right hand sometimes holds your fork
(The wrong hand, those who know would say),
Idly suspended as you talk –

The way I always have. A pen
I similarly use. As light
Procures the page it shows again
Not how we speak but how we write.

The love of friends – from every school –
Defines us, not by etiquette,
But by a law more durable,
Made, not in heaven, or, not yet.

20 November 1990

December 1990

This is not a poem
about leaves
            or the way
the wind huffs them across
the brittle terraces
of light
            that climb the day –
nor transience of chrome –
refractile ambers
                        browns –
rather their legacies –
cast in the paving stones
these random shapes.
                        We tread
indelible shadows –
the streets
            colder like these
are populous as towns.

December 1990

1991

The Joke

The day turns in its cage
    And urgent people run,
Hysterical with rage,
    Under a dying sun.

Through every roaring street
    Inhuman voices try
Their anthem of defeat.
    Words blacken the sky.

A siren cuts the dark.
    And no one has the time
To love or make his mark –
    Each his own paradigm.

The citizen must borrow
    What each day will revoke.
Tomorrow or tomorrow,
    It's all a sordid joke.

January 1991

Poem

And I am also this water
                     and this rock,
And these furled leaves, that twist out
                     and become my hands.
I am the root of the first tree,
                     and a new forest –
The soil runs in my veins, seeking
                     its own river.
Walking through rain I can touch you,
                     for you wet my skin.
And we fall into step as you cross a street
                     in another city,
Or turn at the door of your own house,
                     where I also live.

February 1991

Airborne

Over the wheeling lip of clouds
Where light hangs valleys as it catches

Two straight wings as frail as matches,
Flinging currents tear through shrouds

Of confidence in solid ground.
I hear death's engines cranking round.

My ears are made of glass. One eye
Dazzles its bullet at the sky.

A man in uniform says 'Eat' –
A box of goodies, something sweet

To take away the taste of death
That blows its chlorine through the aisles.

The future gapes. I choke for breath.
Down, let me down. I die for miles.

April 1991

Spring Poem

for Jeremy Trafford

If you are by nature green,
enjoying a tendency
to bear foliage, you may
now be well pleased with yourself.

Narcissus poeticus,
local even in cities,
be especially joyful.
Even a determined grouch –
one for whom piles of dead leaves
are the ultimate turn-on –
acknowledges your being
with a twinge of gratitude.

Dominant in our woodlands.
Endymion nonscriptus,
perennial harbinger
of a temperate future
and long walks in important
silence, you may consider
your come-back a sensation.

Forsythia, what can I say …

Human, let us try to be
comparably generous
with our natural talents,
being as vulnerable,
and equally disinclined
to turn away from the sun.

April 1991

The View

Under the window
      man in the evening
            moving through branches
swollen with blossom –
      dream Arcadia
            briefly. Listen, a
lowing of engines
      down to the river
            counters your silence –
bent to a shadow
      cast and foreshortened
            by the same action –
knotting a shoelace
      over the question –
            whether to accede
to inchoate night
      or turn back the hour –
            walk in albedo,
each stone that measures
      and weighs a footstep
            rendered crystalline –
or to stay merely.
      indefinitely,
            at the minute's edge.

May 1991

Hawthorn

Circumbendibus –
a corkscrew, thorny-branched
Crataegus.
      Flexing on
a cantilevered root,
the musculature aches
under its chain of may.

Old fogey in the brake,
itchy with leaves – a bumpkin
rummaging the hedge –
a few spare twigs will do
to deck the window round,
cut from the vital grain
where generous spirits move.

June 1991

The Break

Night-sweat –
                    the cold shock –
A door blown out,
Banging across the deck
Of the nightmare boat
Where I run, seasick,
Out of the rolling bar
Into incredible rain,
Fall through the black air –
And half wake, shivering,
As I hit the sea.
                    My tongue
Cuts on a silent shout,
With a dry side-trick
That works my levered eye.

The room. Half-light
Barely delineates
A chair – transmogrifies
The pattern that repeats
Ingenious plumes along
The height of the far wall
To grotesque hieroglyph –
Weird totems that conceal
Some runic epitaph.

I clench, unclench my mind.
All senses charge, engage
The neural machinery
Of limbs, fingers, a hand:
My pulse tingles.
                    I see
The curtain taking edge,
Through gradations of blond,
To substantivity.

The dream breaks on the day.
Guessing it's five a.m.
Or so, I hear outside
The plangent interplay
Between traffic and bird,
And recognise the same
Dull panic and dismay.

I lift the single sheet.
What is the world doing?
And what does this light mean?
In case some miracle
Is working in the street,
I rush to the window, lean
Right out over the sill.
Nothing to report.
It must have rained. That's all.
Just colder than I thought.

July 1991

Ardèche, August 1991

Past the house, a shading ash,
handfuls of staining berries
we could turn into wine with know-how –
mountains – the bluish colls
whose wooded sides
harbour the drift, dark,
of a cloud's mirror.
                        A single wasp,
forth and back with its burden
of wood-pulp (the small table,
my vase of beer in the shade).

I ask and you say the river.
Two syllables fall through the light,
return the question: How to stay this time –
harder to quantify
hours that do not pass – how to atone …

Any moment now,
cicadas, a word from the leaves.

August 1991

Station Buffet, Ipswich

In light grey jeans shorn off above the knee,
With cotton sleeves rolled up, strong boots cross-laced,
He's dressed for some adventure out of doors.

His girl companions watch me watching him –
Bizarre collusion in desire's exchange
He's too engrossed in reading to observe.

His focus alters as he turns a page,
Courting distraction with an upward glance
That takes in half the room. Instinctively

I shift my gaze onto the farther wall,
Steady my thought-train on its ringing lines,
And catch him waving in a bright cartoon.

August 1991

Safe Sex

We meet in the interstices of dreams –
Behind the bike-sheds north of Erebus –
In back rooms and dark alleys of the mind.

I hold to every pulse – his, his, my own –
Stare through his eye and endlessly appraise
The metamorphoses of a nameless god.

Our nights are epic, vanished in a turn
That pulls me out of sleep, awed like a child
Claiming his hero with the first embrace.

September 1991

End of Season

It pulls again, a green wave at my heels,
Furling the summer under, and it feels
Significantly colder. Day by day
The light renounces, as it falls away,
Its rash investments: each redundant leaf
Hangs an ironic comma. A kind of grief –
No arbitrary conventional despair –
Wells at the edge of reason, corrupts the air:
Profound incontrovertible dis-ease,
And death of love. The rain burns in the trees
That stand in Kensington, filling the park
With tattered banners. The Albert Hall is dark
Where the new Britons invoked Jerusalem –
Who knew that it would not be built for them –

Sang out their hearts. To those who did not hear,
Lacking all senses but the sense of fear
That breaks at day, the legacies of drink,
The agony of trying not to think,
When the long night bolts its iron to the walls,
And petrifies a city as it falls.
The pavement turns the colour of the sky.
Look up through old leaves. Watch as the stars die.

October 1991

The Dancing Partner

Forty odd years ago you nearly died,
When, as you turned, a bullet brushed your teeth
Leaving behind a taste like nicotine.
In retrospect a shocking accident,
Though, seconds later, you were still alert –
The foliage was thorned with bayonets,
The trees fruited with eyes.
                              Burma it was,
Far out of Lancashire and even wetter –
The monsoon dark that glutted in the bone,
The trenches deep with maggots, pencil snakes –
Knowing one afternoon the sudden chill,
The sure prognostic of malaria.
After six months eight out of forty men
Survived to shake the leeches from their boots
And sailed for England, late-comers at the party.

And after it all the continuum of death,
And the endless pointless hanging on, the waste
Of blood and talent in defence of borders –
For heaven is a dry place with no trees,
Or a place of water densely forested,
With good roads that traverse no hostile quarter –
But not here and not now.
                              Stay drunk if you can –
Sleep in your bamboo body till the day.
Sunset and starset, countless numbers fall.

October 1991

The Colour of Trees

in memoriam Eardley Knollys 1902–1991

Behind the blue corolla of your eye,
You wandered in a landscape where the trees
Grew in amazement at your love of them –
Plausibly red, or bronzy where they fell
In a Hampshire wood.
                              High on the fields of Spain,
Alone in the Serrania de Ronda,
You walked for hours in cerulean valleys,
Observed the reinventions of the light
On house-tops, followed the *camino* back,
Through sheer perspective, down the vivid chases
Toward a gallery off West Halkin Street
You hung with branches from al-Ahmar's garden.

November 1991

Invocation at Solstice

Four o'clock dark
Leans on the rail of day,
While hulls of leaf-smoke lift and slide away
Across the park.

That have let fall,
Deciduously made,
Hang in the weft of dusk, but cast no shade
On any wall.

Season of sleet,
When night laces the air
And shakes down the conundrum of its hair
Over the street:

Think of a gift
For each whose hope is killed,
And with the snows, let that affection build
A deeper drift.

December 1991

1992

Brumal

This cold weather
Renders other
That lights farther:
Perceive beyond

The rimed fences
Sunlight lances –
That bright dance is
A sea of land.

A quinquereme
Laden with brume
Trawls in the loam,
Makes aqueous

The nearest field:
Standing, a child,
Drowned in his world,
Oblivious.

January 1992

High Force

Light's elver-fury of terrible water,
A hawser-thrash across these Pennine shoulders –
Through Caldron Snout, under the Cronkley Scar,
And rocks that brace against its wild kinetics –
Past high ground where the Celtic hunter-farmers
Had laboured in their windy settlements,
And down the bastions of shale and whinstone
In a flight of whips.
                                    Growing in thunder,
The juniper and mealy primula –
And at the watershed blue gentians
Still prove the radiance of a timid fuse.

January 1992

A Valentine

If, other than the heart –
Which barely signifies
A portion of its art –
        I could devise

Some potent metaphor,
That would so well express
My love, what should I draw
        That you might guess?

Having no graphic skill,
My medium is the word –
Trusting its voice is still
        The least absurd.

February 1992

Vertigo

In a dream of black bee-swarms, I came
To a wood's edge in search of a hiding place.
The trees grew tall and densely – birch and ash,
Sweet chestnut, also the lower shrubs.
In a clearing – ivy-bordered and gloomy
With umbrage – I paused, sensing under foot
A tremor in the root-stock: out of the glebe,
In a helix, with a raucous grating of stones
And a rending of foliage, there broke a case
Of stairs. And though a presentiment held me,
I heard the fizzing of the wings and the fury
Of my pursuers.
                              Two steps at a time,
I found myself beyond the tilt of leaves
And clambered through an hour.
                                        At the night's edge –
Gradations of a dark cyanic broadened
To a ceiling fixed with bright amorphous points –
I came to a locked door. And a sudden terror,
Cold in my plexus, flung its shackles round me:
The spiral had corroded and I fell –
Through fields and oceans and the hearts of cities,
Into a desert at the edge of London.
I saw the lights of death's pantechnicon,
And my cold bed that rocks at the brink of day.

January–February 1992

S. W. 5

Pigeons are mating on a window-sill
Above the traffic in the Earl's Court Road.
We dare not risk such informality,
But have a way of looking and a code:
        Owning no feathers,
        We sport our leathers.

March 1992

The Departure Lounge

'He's gone to the departure lounge,' you said –
Meaning, of course, he had not long to live.
Your tone was serious. I smiled instead,
Struck by the metaphor you chose to give
The irreversible process of decline
In one you must have loved (in your own way),
And how a quirk of speech can redefine
The real sense of loss.
                              Now, every day,
The faces have grown thinner round the bar.
We lose each other and we have not met –
Our separation ever more bizarre,
Based as it is on mutual regret,
Ironic in its total unity.
Death and the fear of death, of sensual fraud,
Darken the private chambers of the city
That echoes, like a vast communal ward,
With a dry-throated rage.
                              Clenching our pills,
We leave our doctors, newly diagnosed,
Think only of the virus that it kills
And how much to confide – or are composed,
Armed with a clearer knowledge as we chance
A cool controlled reaction: I recall
Profound relief, a kind of arrogance.
I had not reckoned that the sky would fall.

March 1992

The Reunion

In my last nightmare, Gary Jones,
The faceless councillors had built
One vast estate across the northern hills –
A labyrinth of unadopted streets
Without provision for a single wood,
Where playgrounds lay unmarked, four acres square,
That had been reservoirs,
Their walls inclined and set with broken glass.

In my last nightmare, Gary Jones,
You were the gentle reaver at my side –
Through rain-dark red-brick terraces,
My vandal brother.
We were young-old as the gangs
Pursued us, shouting, but afraid of you –
My father's name
Loud in their teeth, their hands
All red around the stones that weighed their pockets.
– Young-old and strangers when we reached
A quarry's edge, flung backwards by the wind:
'This is the place,' you said. 'You will be safe
Among these rocks.'

                    On our last day at school,
When you ran past me through the wire-mesh gate –
Friend, at the last, of all my enemies –
I wept all down the long hill back
By unknown ways,
And could not recognise my mother's house.

March 1992

Heavy my Gold-ball Baby

for my hamster

Heavy my gold-ball baby,
The swing of my waking –
Night had rocked me under,
Safe in his oubliette.

Blood-thing in a soft clench,
Dreaming your wiry house –
Poor toy, my little pet,
So still and listening –

Is it a failing echo,
The lament of the genus,
That calls to this dim corner
So far from Syria?

March–April 1992

April Shower

The April rain irradiates the street,
Beading the curtained sunlight at the door.
No one I know walks in. A song begins.
I can't think why I come here any more.

The surly kid who's managing the bar
Fondles a ring of keys: he used to be
The glass-collector here. Promoted since,
He checks the progress of a camp trainee

Whose looks are perfect, though he cannot pull
His pints and won't survive a week of this.
One of the old boys waves a twenty note
And orders gin and tonic with a kiss.

He's got his eye on something for the evening –
This bleachy kitten sporting mucky pumps –
And wonders how to get him back to Bromley.
The laser in the CD player jumps.

It's time to go. My glass brims with the glare
From the wet pavement. I never liked this tune.
The barboy lisps we'll see you later. Maybe.
If he's still here tomorrow afternoon.

April 1992

To the Wild Cherry Trees

Song as I live and breathe,
Help me to love this day,
Knowing my host may rise
And will not let me stay

To gather my vague ambitions
In your branches like birds –
These untidy phrases,
A few homeless words.

I cannot hold this fear,
Nor can I come to terms
With the reality of death
Each morning reaffirms:

I watch the cherry trees
Unfurl fresh buds of pain.
Now they have touched the sun,
Tomorrow they are rain.

April 1992

Scene in May

Over the bark-brown walls
The sun rolls down its heat –
Leaf-gleam and plashing light
Fall through the lolling furls –

Under whose tented wave
The road is glade and gold –
A garden in the world
Where wings and shadows move.

May 1992

The Return

Returning from an arid land
(All night her olive groves
Had stirred under the *suspiro de Moro*)
I saw the evening lay a blue-grey arm,
Embankment to embankment, on the Thames.
Half-traced, the colour of the sky,
My image in the window of the train,
A grave transparency.
                    Victoria:
A village with a station –
Gate of the city, where I was set down
Among the lost commuters of the world:
I tried to speak but found no dialect,
Hearing a cry that shook the continent.
And London sighed to far Andalusia –
Across her mountains and the shouting seas –
As if no other language could express
The fear in the blood of the people,
The agony of the waters,
Of roots that suffer in the grieving earth.

June 1992

Unscheduled Stop

I sit in the *Charles Hallé*
At windy Manningtree,
While gulls enact their ballet
Above the estuary.

'We seem to have some problem …'
A faltering voice explains.
I spy, along the platform,
A sign: 'Beware of Trains'

And picture you, impatient,
In the car-park at the back
Of a gaudy toy-town station,
Or craning down the track,

As the afternoon rehearses
An evensong of birds –
Our time in the hands of others,
And too brief for words.

June 1992

The Bed

Waking to sallow light,
I shift position in
the comfortable hard
bed I have made in my
unrestful sleep a place
of tangled warmth that still
feels dampish where the sheet
exposes hand and arm.

All night my body tried
to mend its blood and wept
a lamina of sweat
through its integument –
that once so live it burned
to hold and gratify
the naked strength it sought –
to tear itself apart.

July 1992

For Parvin and Michael Laurence

'… she was thankful to come to rest in such a beautiful place.'
Olivia Manning, *The Spoilt City*

I did not know her, but I'd guess
Olivia would have approved
Of this reunion of friends –
Drawn close to where her ashes lie
Under a quilt of marguerite.
But this is not an elegy
For one who thought this island blest,
And found it beautiful to die:
Rather, I celebrate this house,
That welcomed her in life and death,
And two whose genius excels
At simple generosity.

Thanks then to Michael and Parvin,
Whose home at Billingham was once
Haven for smugglers, and the scene
Of a tragic duel for rival love;
Not far, the keep of Carisbrooke –
Last refuge of a fated king.
Perhaps his ghost is watching here
With your lost friend, Olivia,
As we, your guests, depart her grave,
Raise to the living every glass,
And walk into a garden where
The sun lights on the singing leaves.

July 1992

At the Lake

No god has made him but the sun
Has rolled invisible leaves of fire
Across his shoulder blades and down
His lean long body. Round his feet,
The lake is slung in glinting lines,
Bound for the shadows of his hands.

Lac de Castelgaillard, France
August 1992

The Scaffolders

Before I fall awake,
    they have begun to raise
one level of the structure that will take
        a full two days
        to make complete
round three sides of the house across the street.

    Hot, naked to the waist,
        one of athletic build
stands halfway as the hollow rods are placed:
        he is so skilled –
        his almost-dance
a part of action, risk, the love of chance.

    Intrepid acrobats –
        becoming, as they climb
into their element, agile as cats.
        Taking his time,
        one gets so high,
he whistles as his shoulders brush the sky.

August 1992

All Day the Rain

All day the rain
Drags at the light of things. Especially
At these: the burned-out flares,
Shot from the wound in the heart of genius,
To flash, minutely red, disconsolate,
And die in the cornea.
                              Everywhere,
Always in silence, always
Without effect, knowing he will fall down,
Man weeps to man,
And is afraid of rain. – Or because the sky
Harbours indifference, shaking its cloud
In a black fist, over a scrawl of trees.
– He is ashamed, because the leaves keep falling –
Always in silence, always
Finding himself alone in the same street,
That has no birds.
                              All day the rain
Drags at the light of things.

September 1992

Green Fingers

I cleave from the live stem
Its petiolated leaf –
A pearled ellipse,
Divided by the darker midrib. Here,
A tap-root will emerge,
Through water in a glass.
I love its bright potentiality –
The pattern of these veins –
A miracle
Charges the nucleus.

But look how the green world
Lies burning at the feet of men.

September 1992

September Journey

Eastbound under a crag-dark sky –
Bouldering clouds
Have massed over the train, its girdered wheels
Ground shudderingly still,
Between London and the sea. Down on the bank,
Wet flowers of autumn weed
Glow by the track. Dense intercoiling stems
Explore the alien steel, testing a sleeper,
Or scrabble their tendrils in the loose chipped stone –
Seeming, as they encroach,
To multiply.
                Is it this live machine –
The slung reticulated wires,
Its wheels like trellises –
They touch for? Do they sense
A keener radiance – the warmth of skin?
What if the trees
Dartled with yellow fire –
Lean down dark garages of leaves,
Locking their crankled roots across the rails?

The soil has judged us.
                Then ask forgiveness:
For the burning of the forest,
For the murder of the creatures,
And the poison in the river,
And of the rain, that hangs
In bouldering clouds, under the crag-dark sky.

October 1992

The Turning Circus

for Jenny MacKilligin

Drunk in the afternoon,
I sip the expensive wine
In a bar off Hanover Square,
Next to a kangaroo vine
And three men talking money
Over continental lager.

Convinced that he is funny –
Recounting a late lost bet
On the age of a colleague –
One loosens his collar to let
The heat of his fervour escape him
As he starts the story over.

These three belong here completely –
Deaf, in their rising elation,
To the song in the wind at the window;
The lament of a generation
For whom the city was furnished
With infinite promise of fortune.

Hard cash is cold currency; yet
We inhabit a state to be cherished –
In our separate worlds we can savour
The tang of an over-priced claret,
Or continental lager,
Reassured that, at least, we deserve it.

And we never need talk to each other,
And there'll always be someone to blame.
And perhaps I will sit here for ever,
For the night is a turning circus,
And the wind outside will never
Let us forget our shame.

But, dear, I am coming to meet you,
Inside the appointed doorway.
We'll ride in a glittering taxi
Around the turning circus,
And always talk to each other.
And the wind shall repeat our story.

October 1992

Early November

The day was gold early and I went out under the wind
Over the vivid leaves as they were singing in whispers –
A high day with a blue brim riding over the roof-backs,
Leaving the trees red in amazement at their own brightness.
Down Piccadilly to the Circus on a sleek fourteen,
I went, in my long coat, into the loud heart of the town,
Alighted, danced with several people, kissed one that I knew
Whose cheek was blushed with cold, called at a bar in Poland Street,
And overheard the discourse of a dozen thirsty souls.

The day was old early and I went back in sudden rain
Under the lamps, by windows flushed with light in upper rooms,
Among the people dancing out of offices and stores
Into the brilliant streets and the cool ballroom of evening,
Over the dark-drowned leaves as they were singing in whispers.

November 1992

Sleep, Spirit, in your Branching Bed

Sleep, spirit, in your branching bed,
Lie down under the lawns and spread
A frost over your fallen dead.
The hands of stars meet overhead –
Sleep, spirit, in your branching bed.

November 1992

The Field

Above the once industrial town,
Where necessary buildings stand –
Brick houses in the eighties style,
The same but for diversely painted doors –
There used to be a field,
A graveyard and a ruined church;
Lilac and blackthorn, jungles of meadow-sweet.

Close to my mother's house,
And far enough away
From the dark mansion where I went to school,
This was my refuge, all my universe.

Among the long-untended graves
Of Watsons, Jacksons, Cleggs –
Narcissus and wild daffodils,
Useful on birthdays (more exotic gifts
Came from our neighbour's garden) and below,
Luminous ranks of rose-bay willow-herb:
Food for the hawk-moth lava; in September,
A drift of seeds.
                    One special friend
Was welcome there – a big rough girl
Called Alison, who fought
Most of my battles. An average gang of boys,
Discouraged by her size and wrestler's gait,
Would never have believed
Her gentle way with animals or flowers.

The new estates pile up against these hills,
Their regular gardens fenced and cleared of trees.
In small car parks,
Children are playing electronic games.
I want to tell them certain miracles.

December 1992

The Playground Bell

Dead drunk by nine – this used to be enough.
In Manchester I went out every night;
Picked up and stayed wherever there was drink
With men whose names were last thing on my mind –
Including one who slung the Union Jack
Over his bedside lamp for atmosphere
On the Last Night of the Proms in eighty-two;
My first 'experience': even the white socks
I'd been advised to wear were a success –
One foot displayed, half-casually, to mark
My absolute virginity. The final touch:
My mother fixed a blow-wave in my hair.

Always indulgent towards her only son
(Lucky for me my parents got divorced),
She must have sensed I wasn't the same boy
Who'd walked for twenty miles or more a day
On gritstone tracks, over the backs of hills –
The Pennine wastes of Bleaklow, Kinder Scout.

The landscape of the city was more harsh:
Bleaker than any tract of mountain peat,
The bus ride down the Manchester Old Road.
In Sackville Street, between the Thomson's Arms
And the Rembrandt Hotel, a universe
Peopled by drunks and rent boys – one a punk,
Who used to leave his girlfriend at the bar
On business. After barely half an hour,
He'd stroll back in and stand them both a drink.

I quickly learned the language and the code –
Had 'sisters' who were kind men twice my age,
Who paid for beers and thought I was mature;
Confided, gave advice and lent me fares.
On Saturday nights we'd drive to Liverpool
Or Stoke-on-Trent, as if there were a difference
Between one seedy night-spot and another –
Though local accents used to turn me on,
And that rare prize – a genuine foreigner
On holiday – was worth the taxi ride
To some remote hotel. Leaving in secret,

Before breakfast, pocketing an address
(In Paris!) I would never write to, a poignant act.

One Christmas I saved up and went to Heaven –
The biggest dive in England, under Charing Cross –
A three-tiered circuit ranged by packs of men,
And boys who came to dance. I ended up
In a basement somewhere off the Chepstow Road,
And woke to the first snowfall of the year.
I came to London for a long weekend
And stayed: met someone famous who was kind,
And took a boring job in Portland Place.
I went, on summer nights, to Hampstead Heath,
Where pints of beer at Jack Straw's Castle gave
To sex under the tents of holly trees –
Shadows of hands that flowered through the dusk:
No names, no contracts, but each parting hug
Was less a token of civility
Than an act of love.
                              Later, in Amsterdam,
In crowded cellars on the Warmoesstraat,
The rules were different – a more serious art,
Practised in uniform. The smell of leather
An aphrodisiac keen as the scent of leaves;
And still, the magic of indifference.

It still goes on – wherever hands can find
Response of hands; hold, in the hollow silence,
A tangible warmth, the heartbeat in the dark
Where death has entered, ringing the playground bell.
It hurts the ear. It echoes through the woods.

I stare at death in a mirror behind the bar
And wonder when I sacrificed my blood,
And how I could not recognise the face
That smiled with the mouth, the eyes, of death –
In Manchester, London or Amsterdam.
I do not hate that face, only the bell.

December 1992

1993

Hammersmith, Excuse Me

for my mother

'*Dance in the old-fashioned way*,' croons Aznavour,
From two colossal speakers in mid-air.
Unwanted chaperon, I fetch the tea
In polystyrene cups. As I return

The Latin King is holding out his hand –
An invitation to a lilting rumba.
You smile acceptance and with *Spanish Eyes*
Go turning in your starry element.

You're up for every number – *California Blue*,
The Breeze and I and *Lady is a Tramp*.
I sit among the ranks of single men,
Moved by your art – the energy and grace

Inherent in each step, practised for years
At Blackpool Tower; in grand Mancunian halls.
An average floor, you say: but I'm impressed,
As you disco with a man who's twice your size

(It's *Boogie Woogie Bugle Boy* this time) –
And wonder if the kids on Friday night
Feel half your joy in living, are aware
That one quick step is often all it takes.

January 1993

Edvard Munch

The shadow of the window on the floor –
A double cross cast by the moon,
Night in St Cloud – lengthens from where he sits,
Your friend, the poet, indistinct except
For sinister top hat
And one arm propped against the window pane.
But now it's you –
Painter of the agonising stillness
In the death chamber –
Mourning your sister by the dark river,
In a Paris suburb far from Christiana.

Another room: a frail pubescent girl –
Her shadow on the wall behind,
A huge black phallus, looms above the bed.
Horror contracts her shoulders and these eyes –
Mirrors of inexperience that stare
Into the staring faces of the crowd –
That *Evening on Karl Johan* – or, confused,
Follow the dance at Åsgårdstrand,
Where a smiling woman
Lifts up her lovely hand, impossibly,
Towards love's flower. Her counterpart, in black –
Excluded, motionless –
Looks on in anguish as the moon presides.
– Again it's you –
Painter of the rejection on the shore,
Of kisses that destroy,
Who heard, at sunset, from the dark blue hills,
An endless scream filling the sky with blood.

A vampiress, a sensual Madonna,
Love bears her ashes to your grave.
Cold in your fist, a broken heart –
Your vision of eternity, its flower.

January 1993

In the Garden

I

Dream-deep and heavy
The swing of my waking –
Night had rocked me under,
Safe in her oubliette.

I come back slowly,
Out of a broken landscape
And a deserted dwelling.
This was my mother's garden –
Its blue gate on a string,
And the mock-orange tree
Weighted with halves of bricks.
Strange detail.
                    But already,
What brought me to this place
Relinquishes, draws back –
Blurring all context.
                            It is
As if I had not dreamed
But seen: for an instant only,
To have been real there.

I lift the gate, falling
Forward into daylight.

II

This ground is difficult.
Old walls are buried here.
I have a spoon, a rusted nail
And my two hands.
                        I am planting
Nasturtium seeds – when they have grown
I can eat them. The best part
Is the sweet spur behind
The flower.
                    Digging is fun –
                            the smell of soil.

This is my patch of ground, between the gate
And the mock-orange tree.
Here I shall plant whatever I can find —
Something with sturdy roots
That comes up every year.

I found a lump of marble in the yard —
It might be useful.
                    If I build
A miniature landscape, this rock
Could be a mountain.
                            I had better clear
Space for a forest with my little spoon.

III

Darkness commend them to a track of leaves
Who love their shape. Let the dark forms impose
A tense half-fallen stillness, where the blood races
Through wings of lovers in the veils of grass.

Tonight, in this cool place by a velvet river,
Hands meet in the sound of the amen of water —
Here, where breathless woods return the whisper
Of heart to fiery heart through the dense cover.

Walk with me to the gate of a quiet garden,
Where scents of invisible flowers compound and deepen —
Holding each other, finding the gate open,
While people among the shadows rise and beckon.

Under the leaves, by this cool watershed,
Alone together we shall make our bed.

IV

O brothers, sisters —
Look how the garden fills
With too much light,
And how the rain
Burns in the crown
Of the mock-orange tree.

Beyond the gate,
The garden of the world –
Observe the extent
And impact of our works:
The ocean rises
At the delta.

That sound, that sound
Is the screaming
In the forest –
The rending of timber
And the dispossession
Of the creatures.

In the cold hills
Above the city
A child leans on his gun.
Elsewhere, he starves to death
And has no burial
In the dry ground.

Murder and rape
Are the inheritors.
We have no language
And nothing is audible
But the machinery
Of vengeance.

O brothers, sisters –
Look how the grass withers,
How the stream vanishes –
Look how the rain
Burns in the crown
Of the mock-orange tree.

February 1993

Island Visit

for David Gascoyne

Drank a gin coming down –
Fast out of Waterloo.
Mainland gusty in blondshine,
Then, light-bound on Solent water,
Bladed with sun, my boat bumps at the harbour.
I see you in front of the sky, with Judy, waving.

Later, in the glare
Of your front living room,
After a simple lunch,
You show me some of the books
You could not live without – Pierre Jean Jouve –
Treasure from Parton Street or the Rue de l'Odéon.

Discomfited somehow,
You return to your favourite chair,
Who was in love in Paris –
That night in '38
At Place Dauphine under the chestnut trees,
Alone in silence with your *jeune Danois*.

You help me to a drink,
But tell me you must wait
Till seven-thirty sharp –
Relying as you do
On the routine you need to keep you sane,
Having fallen on that *chemin des abîmes*

That led you through the wastes
Of tortuous middle age
And broke you more than once,
Though you survive it seems,
Safe on your island. Tomorrow I return
To a world where you were never at your ease.

You read from Marianne Moore
And seem to take such strength
From images that ring
Like pæans from your lips.
You listen to my poems. As I look up,
A kindling flame disturbs your level gaze.

March 1993

Going North

for Michael Schmidt

Half an hour from Euston and already
The sun, it seems, has travelled far enough,
Preferring the mutable palette of the Thames –
Artful with rooftops and the sides of towers,
Slick in the City, idle in Green Park.
It's odd and a bit depressing, this going north –
Though it's where I started – when I had my health,
And didn't smoke, drank mainly at weekends,
And slept with my first boy.
                    In Stalybridge –
My mother's town, half urban, half serene
With factory woods and desolate canals –
A paradise of walks and *nice old pubs*,
Newt-fishing and the yammering of birds –
And, how could I forget, that bloody school.

It can't be far now. Something about the light
Alters perception of the falling land –
A sense of urgency, of losing time,
As though I'd come without some vital key.
At Crewe the sky turns uniformly grey,
And who can blame it. Further up the line
Old Manchester sits in the cold and waits for rain
That's bound to come – she can feel it in her bones.

Yet it's not the cultural desert I remember
(Though I probably missed a trick or two in my teens)
Or why would you have struck such sturdy roots?
It's good to know you're up here running things,
That we'll have lunch and gossip in *The Italia*.
And yet it never feels like coming home,
Wherever that may be. Perhaps it's where
The heart lies, like a room in Kensington,
In Mexico. The Cheshire fields fly south.
At Jodrell Bank they're talking to the stars.

March 1993

Poem on St Patrick's Day

Woke on St Patrick's Day
From a dream of my own death
Wracked in an old man's body
Under a heavy sheet,
And caught my breath
And lifted off the quilt.

I looked and found you sleeping,
And could not find a name
For what turned in an instant
From waking fear –
Relief? No, not relief.
You are more to me than that.

Half Irish, you
Will celebrate this day
With shamrock in your coat,
Drink after work
And telephone abroad,
Your mother's eldest son.

I lose weight and our bed's
Less comfortable these days.
So, while I can get out,
I'll go down in the light
Of a new season,
To where you are dancing.

March–April 1993

Afterword

Adam Johnson

10 April 1965 – 16 May 1993

It was a cool Wednesday evening in November 1985, and we were gathering at Dillon's to launch the GMP anthology *Not Love Alone*. I'd persuaded a publisher friend, Roger Walton, to lend his moral support: after a couple of drinks in the Museum Tavern, we felt as ready as we'd ever be to face the evening. When we arrived at the bookshop, it turned out that as many of the poets included as were present – half a dozen or so of us – were to read, in alphabetical order, once the publisher's plonk had done its work. What I hadn't anticipated was that this particular alphabet would end with P. Listening to the others, I decided we'd better finish with something a bit substantial, scrapped my planned two or three short pieces, and chose instead a single solid poem called 'Studies'. It seemed to go down well enough, and afterwards two members of the audience – a strikingly attractive boy and his blond friend – approached me: 'That was the only real poem anyone's read this evening,' said the friend (he may have said the same to others). I thought of Auden's encounter with those two students in New York, his famous exclamation to Isherwood: 'It's the wrong blond!'

But if Chester Kalman was the right blond, so was Adam Johnson. His friend, not keen on poetry, vanished; while he joined Roger and me on a cheerful trek to the Lamb and Flag. He'd dressed with a sort of Oxfam elegance, had a face in which the child and the old man were simultaneously present. He was very conscious of that: at some point in the evening, he asked us to guess his age. Tactfully, we both gave the reply which those younger and older tend to find equally flattering: late twenties. Well, he said, I'm *almost* twenty-one. He asked if he could send me his poems: thinking nothing would come of it, I agreed.

A few days later, they arrived, accompanied by a letter (dated 15 November) as quaintly formal as Adam's taste in clothes: 'As I promised, I enclose a selection of my completed verse for your perusal,' it began. He looked forward to 'some valuable criticism and good advice' (which I'm relieved to see I did my best to provide) and to 'our next meeting and a hearty chat'. The poems themselves, though marred by archaisms and generalities, were promising – in the exact and exciting sense of that word so often employed as a euphemism for 'not much good'. Amazingly, he took notice of my more sensible comments, as the revised versions in his privately-printed pamphlet

In the Garden (1986) demonstrate. His willingness to listen, rejecting advice as well as accepting it, and his ability to learn constantly from his own reading were crucial factors in his remarkable development as a poet.

And one 'hearty chat' led to another, in London pubs or at my home in Hertfordshire. During one of them, we decided that I'd give up the teaching job I'd had for a dozen years and start, from scratch, a bookshop. He came as my guest to the staff party at the end of the summer term, which then seemed daring even in a so-called 'progressive' school, and charmed almost everyone. He said he'd work on the bookshop, and did: the whole place was derelict, with a flat above but the kitchen on the ground floor at the back. I remember him happily assembling kitchen units in the huge living-room, only to discover that, once assembled, they wouldn't fit down the staircase. He'd come up for weekends once we'd opened and help out on Saturdays. On his first morning, an imposing woman came to the counter with several books. 'I'll just find a bag for you,' he said, unsure where things were, 'for the books, that is, not for you.' 'You'd need a bag on wheels to put me in, young man,' she said. From that day, Bag-on-Wheels became one of my most loyal customers, and she always asked after Adam. Later in that autumn of 1986 he moved in.

He wouldn't have called Baldock his home, of course, nor anywhere else until his last years in Redcliffe Gardens: he was like a peripatetic cat with known staging-posts for food, shelter and affection. Occasionally, again with cat-like inscrutability, he'd vanish altogether – to Amsterdam or Copenhagen or London. He'd created around himself a degree of spacial freedom which enabled him constantly to meet new people, ranging from boys in bars to an impressive number of literary and musical acquaintances. At first, I thought he was cynically filling his address-book, but I was wrong: it was part of a perpetual hunger for knowledge and experience. Long before he knew for certain that he was HIV positive, he lived with hectic urgency, as if on borrowed time: he used to say he'd die of cancer before he was thirty.

Partly for that reason, his work developed rapidly too. He had the good sense to bury his juvenilia in subsequently inaccessible places – self-published pamphlets and fugitive bits of the gay press. Only when he'd worked through an early phase of anger and propaganda did he begin seriously to approach the literary magazines and publishers where a reputation might be made: his poems started to appear in mainstream magazines like *Acumen* and *Outposts* and then, to his great delight, in *PN Review*; he prepared a slim collection, *The Spiral Staircase*, for Acumen and a more substantial one, *The Playground Bell*, for

Carcanet. In retrospect, it's clear that he was mapping out his literary career with a good deal of judicious care.

He had a sure instinct for the poetic occasion: so many of the poems are about his encounters and travels, often carrying affectionate dedications to friends across the dinner table or at the journey's end. In August 1991 he even wrote a poem while stuck between trains in the station buffet at Ipswich; it was drafted – but, with so scrupulous a writer, certainly not 'finished' – by the time he reached Saxmundham. Though his subject-matter was predominantly urban, he wrote marvellously on the natural world, as in 'Hawthorn' ('Old fogey in the brake, / itchy with leaves – a bumpkin / rummaging in the hedge') or 'High Force' ('Light's elver-fury of terrible water, / A hawser-thrash across these Pennine shoulders') or, closer to home in Earl's Court, 'Early November':

> The day was gold early and I went out under the wind
> Over the vivid leaves as they were singing in whispers –
> A high day with a blue brim riding over the roof-backs,
> Leaving the trees red in amazement at their own brightness.

He was deeply attentive to nature: in Suffolk, where I'd moved in 1990, he'd discover fungi (he could name them all) in the birch-woods, spiders presiding over their webs on the gorse, and – in April 1993, on his last visit – dozens of tiny pastel-coloured snails in the marshes. Like Hardy, 'He was a man who used to notice such things.'

One day early in 1992 he said to me: 'By the way, they're not calling it HIV any more.' The effect on him was a kind of quintessential distillation or concentration: after all, he'd always had the sense of living and working against the clock. He wrote, with even greater urgency, his best poems. Some – 'The Bed', for instance, and 'The Playground Bell' – are very specifically about Aids; but by then he had learnt the power of reticence and decorum, so that the poems simultaneously address the universal theme of man confronting his mortality. The final one he completed, 'Poem on St Patrick's Day', for Jim Lovendoski, with whom he spent his last five years, ends with a characteristically wry stoicism:

> I lose weight and our bed's
> Less comfortable these days.
> So, while I can get out,
> I'll go down in the light
> Of a new season,
> To where you are dancing.

His courage was extraordinary and utterly self-effacing. In December

1992, he came with me to a reading I was giving in Norwich; thinking about the poems before we set out, I started to ask: 'Do you mind if I read …?' 'I *want* you to read "A Virus",' he said firmly. I'd written that poem shortly after his HIV status had been confirmed. At the end of the reading, a man in the audience rebuked me for taking these things too seriously: I felt murderous, but Adam produced his gentlest ironic smile.

Sometimes he affected an unlikely leather-boy persona (he said he'd found the jacket abandoned on a dustbin) or, more commonly, a style of equally absurd foppish decadence. Both were masks. Intellectually, he had more in common with the sixteenth century than with the nineteenth or perhaps even the twentieth. Hence his openness to literary influence: you could often see in Adam's poems what he'd been reading last week, just as you can in Shakespeare's or Jonson's or Donne's. His wit, too, was essentially Elizabethan – verbally acute, punning, frequently obscene yet seldom merely dirty. Words, and the tricks words play, could grow into long-running games: I remember driving with him back from Little Gidding early in 1988, our progress impeded by a barely-moving horse-box in a narrow lane. 'Perhaps its paws are sticking out the bottom and it's pushing the Land Rover,' I said. 'But horses don't have paws.' 'Well, it must be a cat-box, then.' 'Horse-flap.' 'Cat-chestnut.' 'Horsekin.' 'Cat-and-cart.' And so on. An invaluable invention for long journeys, our animal game, with its endless and increasingly ludicrous zoological permutations, often spontaneously hi-jacked our conversations – frequently in pubs, to the bemusement of barmen and bystanders.

Above all, there was music. He knew as much about music – as with literature, his brilliant self-education was a constant reproach to academic cultural monopoly – as anyone I have ever met. His knowledge was absolutely practical: on almost any work from Mozart onwards (his expertise hadn't yet stretched to early music), he'd produce an instantaneous comparison and recommendation of performances, a sort of walking *Good CD Guide*. He was the ideal concert-going companion, too. Halfway through the oddly lacklustre CBSO performance of Mahler 9 at the 1991 proms, we exchanged grimaces: 'He's up to something,' said Adam, and with that, Rattle launched ferociously into the third movement followed immediately by the most liquidly elegiac performance of that wonderful concluding Adagio that either of us had ever heard. Mahler, Shostakovich, Britten are the composers I'll always associate with him, but there were occasions which were well beyond that range – a marvellous *Dido and Aeneas* at the 1990 Aldeburgh Festival, the *St John Passion* (which he was hearing for the first time, and loved) at Blythburgh in 1992. When

Rattle and the CBSO (again) recorded Mahler 7 at Snape in 1991, we were there: like Larkin in that poem called 'Broadcast', I try to hear our hands in the applause at the end of the disc.

I wasn't at the funeral, prevented by a conspiracy of British Rail's Saturday timetable and a fallible car. It was a soft, warm, hazily sunny morning: I walked to a quiet spot between the sea wall and the River Alde; there were tiny pale bees on the marsh-flowers, purple vetch and sea-pea, and a few black-headed gulls. It was a better place than a South London crematorium to be with Adam. I miss him not just as a friend but as one of those rare beings who, through their work and their presence, truly sustain a culture: and that is a loss to us all.

NEIL POWELL
June 1993

Index of First Lines

Index of Titles